A Journey through Shimmering Currents

In streams where giggles play,
Tiny dances twist and sway.
Each ripple tells a funny tale,
Of froggy leaps and fishy fails.

Water sprites with pranks in mind,
Chase the shadows, one of a kind.
Splashing laughter fills the air,
With every whirl, they shed their care.

Little whirlpools twist and shout,
Sending ducks into a rout.
Spinning tales of sippy cups,
While tippy-toeing, never ups!

A voyage born from giddy dreams,
Where laughter flows like sunlit beams.
Each wave a chuckle, bright and clear,
As nature's jokes bring joy and cheer.

Luminous Lilies in the Stream

Glowing petals on a whimsical ride,
Riding waves, they glide with pride.
Each one bounces, boldly beams,
Sparking laughter, bursting dreams.

A parade of colors, bright and bold,
Telling jokes that can't be told.
In glistening streams where humor flows,
Joyful whispers, go where no one knows.

Spirals of Tranquility in Motion

Spinning in circles, who knew they'd sway?
Making mischief in a buoyant ballet.
Around and around, a twist of fate,
As giggles and splashes animate.

Drifting slowly, oh what a sight,
Chasing rainbows in pure delight.
In tiny whirlpools, laughter flows,
Where joy in every corner grows.

Iridescent Secrets of the Pool

Glittering orbs with winks to share,
Dancing lightly in the air.
They whisper tales of silly plays,
In sunlit pools, they laugh and gaze.

With a splash, a gleam, a cheer,
Guest stars hopping, never fear.
In this watery comical jest,
Each ripple holds a playful quest.

Original title:
Bubbles in the Current

Author: Lila Davenport
ISBN HARDBACK: 978-1-80587-246-7
ISBN PAPERBACK: 978-1-80587-716-5

Celestial Capsules of Reflection

In the water, laughs collide,
Like tiny ships, they gently glide.
Each one pops, a silly sound,
Joyful chaos all around.

Floating dreams with giggles bright,
Chasing shadows, pure delight.
Swirls of glee in every swirl,
A playground for each boy and girl.

Reflections of Joy in Flowing Waters

When sunshine grins upon the stream,
It twirls and sparkles, what a dream!
Fishy faces bob and play,
Their silly antics on display.

One little fish with shades of blue,
Tried to impress a swan that's new.
With a flip and flop, it lost its track,
Colliding with a floating snack!

The surface ripples, giggles rise,
As turtles tumble, oh what a surprise!
Splashing frolics, a watery jest,
In this wild mix, they find their zest.

Reflections ripple with each delight,
Transforming worries into light.
In flowing streams where laughter reigns,
Every drop reveals joy unchains.

The Dance of Light in the Depths

In depths where sparkles swirl and dive,
Creatures laugh, oh how they thrive!
A jellyfish in disco glow,
Bops to tunes the currents flow.

An octopus in polka dots,
Twists and twirls in funny spots.
He juggles shells, a marvelous sight,
With all his arms, he’s quite the knight!

The seaweed sways, a silly dance,
While fishes frolic, take a chance.
Giggles bubble, joy expands,
As the floor of the ocean makes demands.

Bright rays of sun like confetti fall,
Shining happiness, inspiring all.
Through glimmering depths, they dart and glance,
In the ocean's humor, they take their chance.

Moments Suspended in Fluid Grace

As ducks parade in a wobbly line,
They quack and wiggle, feeling fine.
Water glistens with squeaky sounds,
The marsh a giggle, joy abounds.

The turtle crew takes their slow ride,
Waving at fishies, bubbling with pride.
Each little splashed, a moment to keep,
In shimmering waters, laughs never sleep.

A dragonfly in a wild spin,
Zips through laughter, it’s sure to win.
With every turn and flirty tease,
She dances on air with charming ease.

In gentle waves of playful cheer,
Moments captured, crystal clear.
Fluid joys that float and sway,
Where all the silliness finds its way.

Whispers of Floating Ephemera

Little spheres snug in the stream,
They giggle and swirl in a frothy dream.
With each little hop, they puff and they play,
Tickling the fish as they float on their way.

Watch out for the splash, it’s a slippery game,
As the water tickles but never feels shame.
They whisper sweet secrets, a bubble-icious tune,
While dancing with sunlight beneath the bright moon.

Dance of the Drifting Spheres

Spheres in the stream, what a wild waltz!
Knocking on rocks, they giggle and halt.
Like jesters in water, they bounce with delight,
Spinning around, oh what a sight!

With a flick and a flop, they skitter and slide,
A carnival ride on the water's wide tide.
They whisper and chuckle, oh, isn't it grand?
As they twirl and they tumble, all perfectly planned.

Elysian Orbs on a Water Canvas

Tiny orbs paint the pond with a dash,
Each one a canvas, a swirling splash.
A giggle, a pop, what's coming next?
A journey on water, all blissfully vexed.

They race 'round the lilies, twinkling with glee,
While frogs look on, pondering with tea.
The dance of the orbs, it starts and it ends,
In a whimsical waltz, where laughter transcends.

Chasing the Silvered Cascade

In the gleam of a flow, little spheres do flee,
Chasing the shimmer, so happy and free.
They leap and they giggle, they flutter with cheer,
While bubbles take flight, full of mischief and cheer!

Around the slick bends, they twist and they shout,
As the ripples echo, with giggles about.
With glints in their eyes and a splash in their wake,
They're dancing through waters—come join in the cake!

Secrets of the Liquid Veil

In the depths, the whispers dance,
Fluffy orbs in a merry trance.
They giggle, wiggle, float about,
Squeaky voices, laugh out loud.

Clownfish grinning, join the fun,
Making mischief, one by one.
With a splash, they twirl and dive,
In a world where all seem alive.

Drifting by, a jelly's smile,
Wobbling softly, takes its style.
The seaweed sways, a sway so grand,
As they spin, they take a stand.

Riddles held in ocean's grasp,
The laughing waves, a playful clasp.
Giggles echo through the blue,
Secrets kept, just for a few.

Shoreline Echoes of Brightness

At the shore, a cheeky wave,
Spraying sand, it tries to behave.
Silly shells with hats askew,
Chasing dreams of morning dew.

A crab in shades, so proudly strut,
Dancing sideways, what a nut!
With every flip, it sets the pace,
Laughing loud, it leads the race.

Sunshine sparkles, makes a mess,
On the beach, all wrongs addressed.
Children giggling as they play,
Silly antics brighten the day.

As the tide rolls in and out,
Echoes of laughter, there's no doubt.
Each pebble sings, each wave's a tune,
Calling all to join the swoon.

Glimmers upon the Tidal Surface

In the shimmer, fish flash bright,
Swirling colors, pure delight.
They tease each other, twirl and spin,
In a waltz where all can win.

A playful dolphin leaps ashore,
Leaving giggles, always more.
With a splash, it steals the scene,
Under the sun's bright, gleaming sheen.

Starfish splatter across the rocks,
Ticklish waves, playful knocks.
They stick around, so keen to play,
Joining in the fun today.

The ocean’s mirror, bright and clear,
Reflects mischief, full of cheer.
Each ripple sings an ancient song,
In this world where all belong.

Wandering Pearls in the Tide

Little pearls on a frothy spree,
Rolling around in glee, you see.
Skipping over foam and sand,
Life's a jest, just as it’s planned.

Octopus with a crafty grin,
Paints the ocean, lets the fun begin.
With its ink, it plays a prank,
Giggling softly, no need to thank.

Clams shut tight, but peek and stare,
What's that laughter in the air?
As waves rush in, they sway with glee,
In this carnival of the sea.

Each jolt and swirl brings new delight,
As the tide dances, day turns night.
Wandering gems, they love to glide,
In playful dance, they will abide.

Dappled Surfaces of You and Me

We skitter across the pond,
Our laughter pierces the calm,
Like ducks who can't hold the line,
Just wading in dreams like a psalm.

The sun throws us a wink,
As we dance on the rippling waves,
Chasing shadows with a drink,
While splashing like carefree knaves.

A frog leaps, gives us a wink,
As we swirl in a whirl of cheer,
Each moment, a playful blink,
No worries as we disappear.

With every giggle we share,
The world becomes a bright blur,
In the softest evening air,
We glide, both the stars and her.

Fleeting Elegance on the Tide

The tide brings secrets to play,
As we ride on the crests of fun,
Waves crash, and they cheer 'hooray!',
Who knew drenching could weigh a ton?

Driftwood dances in our dreams,
As jellybeans float on by,
We're pirates on candy streams,
With jellyfish sails in the sky.

With each splash, a giggle rings,
As we claim our joyous place,
The sea hums with buoyant flings,
A wet and wild, silly race.

In this ballet of the brine,
Our laughter swells like the sea,
We twirl, we plunge, oh how divine,
Just two kids, forever free.

The Liquid Heartbeat of Dreams

In puddles of giggles we splash,
Our feet fairies dart and dive,
Every drip is a cheeky flash,
Like mischief that's come alive.

We sail on boats made of leaves,
With the wind as our jolly mate,
Chasing the whims that it weaves,
As our fates intertwine in fate.

A seagull squawks from above,
Our hats float away on a whim,
But we laugh as we rush, oh love,
Making a scene, oh so grim.

With rainclouds chasing the sun,
We twirl, dip, and slide with glee,
Each drop a part of our fun,
In this dance of you and me.

Afloat on Nature’s Graceful Touch

We're sailing on marshmallow skies,
In a boat made of giggles and dreams,
Floating boldly where laughter flies,
As the sun wraps us up in its beams.

The breeze tickles our faces, wild,
As daisies play peek-a-boo close,
We’re nature’s sweet, rambunctious child,
Lost in the silliness we chose.

A squirrel steals our last few snacks,
Thinking he's won a grand prize,
But we just laugh at his little acts,
In this charm where laughter never dies.

With every rustle, whispers bring,
A symphony of silly tweets,
And like the softest murmurs sing,
We dance, where the earth discreetly greets.

Luminous Echoes on a Gentle Wave

In the pond where lilies dance,
A frog hops in with a funny prance.
He dives below with great delight,
Then pops back up, quite the sight!

A fish swims by, with a grin so wide,
Whispers, 'Come join, let’s take a ride!'
They swirl and twirl, a comic show,
A splash of laughter, to and fro.

The sun spills glow on this light spree,
As dragonflies buzz with glee.
They flutter and chase, what a wild chase,
Creating joy in a watery place!

With every ripple, there's a cheer,
The antics here bring smiles near.
Nature's jesters in a bright parade,
In this splashy world, joy is made!

In the Arms of Liquid Serenity

A turtle snoozes beneath a log,
While a duckling slips and togs.
He quacks a tune, a silly beat,
To wake the slumber, oh so sweet!

A wave rolls in, with a plop and a pop,
As seaweed strands do a soft flop.
The seagulls laugh, they can't resist,
At every wave, a comical twist.

The shore is a stage, with shells as props,
Sandcastles rise, then tumble and drop.
And every giggle from the tiny crowd,
Turns the ocean bright and proud!

With drifting thoughts like frothy foam,
They weave a story that's far from home.
In this playful ebb, they find their cheer,
Liquid laughter flows, so sincere!

Timeless Wonders of the Blue

In azure depths, where colors gleam,
A clam pops open, bursting a dream.
It makes a noise, both loud and round,
The fish around roll in the sound!

A dolphin leaps with a joyous flip,
Nose diving down, then on a trip.
He coins a joke that travels fast,
And all the corals snicker at last.

Along the reef, the crabs parade,
Wearing tiny hats, they're not afraid.
They twirl and strut in a wooden show,
Three cheers for antics, 'Hip Hip Ho!'

As currents twirl in a jeweled spin,
The ocean's laughter, where smiles begin.
In every nook, where joy takes form,
The timeless wonders keep us warm!

Twinkling Spirits of the Tide

At dusk the tides begin to play,
The stars above join in their sway.
Flickering lights on the gently crest,
Twinkling spirits, in cosmic jest.

A crab does a tango on the sand,
With funky moves, it's quite the brand!
Around it goes, a merry whirl,
Creating ripples each time it twirls.

The moon winks down with a soft glow,
Encouraging all to put on a show.
They leap and swim, a nightly spree,
In this frolic, wild and free!

As waves wash dreams ashore so bright,
Life feels silly in the starlit night.
Among the echoes, laughter resides,
In every splash, the spirit slides!

The Ethereal Waltz from Below

In the depths where giggles play,
Fish wear glasses, bright and gay.
Shrimp in tux, they sway and spin,
Watch the seaweed's goofy grin.

Jellyfish float like balloons,
Dancing to their silly tunes.
Starfish clapping with their hands,
Making waves with odd demands.

Crabs do cha-chas, oh so sly,
While octopi wave, oh my!
Bubbles pop with every cheer,
Underwater, fun is here.

As seahorses prance and tease,
The clowns of ocean, laugh with ease.
In this realm where jesters thrive,
Life’s a joke: we're all alive!

Echoes of Laughter in Liquid Realms

In the tide, a chuckle swells,
With little clams who tell their spells.
Grown-up fish in silly hats,
Paddle by with giggles, splats.

Anemones wave, jive around,
As sea cucumbers strike the ground.
The dolphins whistle, tales to share,
Bubbles popping everywhere!

A lobster joins, a dance parade,
With narwhals in a masquerade.
They tickle fish from every side,
In a splashy, joyful glide.

With laughter ringing in the waves,
Each creature knows how fun behaves.
The ocean's mirth, a bright delight,
Where giggles echo day and night!

Transient Hues in the Tidal Embrace

With shades of blue that twist and swirl,
Colorful critters in a whirl.
The flounder dons a tutu bright,
Spinning tales in the soft light.

Puffer fish puff, what a sight!
Silly faces, oh what a fright!
Mussels play a game of hide,
As laughter rolls like a happy tide.

Tangs in twists, clownfish duel,
Sea turtles race in a playful fool.
Hidden treasures near the sand,
Granting giggles, hand in hand.

In this realm of mirthful jest,
Every turn puts joy to test.
With a wink and wave, they glide,
Through hues and giggles, side by side!

A Journey Through Glistening Trails

On glistening paths of frothy foam,
Crabs declare they won’t go home.
Eels with wigs, they shimmy tight,
Frogfish guffaw in pure delight.

Tangled seaweed, a tickling maze,
Shrimp throw parties, dance and praise.
With a flip, a splash, and a spin,
Chasing laughter hidden within.

Jellybean fish in cute disguise,
Peek from corals with wide eyes.
They prance and play, oh what a show,
In swirls of fun, they steal the glow.

Through glistening trails, their antics thrive,
In this watery world, we joyfully dive.
With each wiggle and splash, we find,
The funniest friends, one of a kind!

Effervescent Dreams on the Tide

Tiny floats of laughter rise,
Dancing whimsies greet the skies.
A splash of giggles in the rush,
Oh, what a silly, frothy hush!

Waves of chuckles start to swell,
Jokes and jests in salty gel.
Ticklish tides, both bold and bright,
Make surf and fun a sheer delight!

Sprightly dreams on salty trails,
Chasing fish with funny tales.
Swirling whims with bubbles fair,
Leave us grinning everywhere!

The ocean hums with joyful call,
As foam and fun entwine for all.
A bubbly toast to giggly times,
Where laughter flows and joy chimes!

Glistening Ghosts of the Stream

Whisking whispers down the brook,
Tales of giggles, take a look!
Ghostly glimmers skipping nigh,
With each splash, they dance and fly.

Willy-nilly, here they prance,
Mischief calls in watery dance.
Floaty fancies twirl about,
Who knew streams could be so sprout?

Flickering can’t even flow,
As little chuckles steal the show.
A gurgling laugh from granite stone,
Echoes of joy twinkling alone.

When ripples giggle, oh what fun,
Nature’s pranks have just begun!
With every shimmer, jesting play,
A chorus of bright whimsy say!

Celestial Glimmers in the Flow

Starlit giggles on the wave,
Where spacey dreams are bold and brave.
Winking drops that shimmer high,
Laughter rings through night’s sly tie.

Cosmic currents full of cheer,
Wobbling wonders drawing near.
Mirrored stars, they laugh out loud,
As they twirl in a shimmering shroud.

Light-years’ glimmers swish and sway,
Funny shapes on cosmic play.
A navigation of sheer fun,
With each splash, more joy is spun!

Twinkling tales from skies above,
In every drop, a pinch of love.
Steering close to laughter’s heart,
The universe takes part!

Liquid Lullabies and Airborne Joys

Dancing droplets softly sing,
Floating notes of everything.
A melody of swirls and sways,
Leading all the hearts to play.

Twirling dreams that hum and glide,
Carried forth by nature’s ride.
Rippled tunes from stream to sea,
Where every splash brings glee, carefree!

Laughter spills in every drop,
A playful jest that won’t stop.
With each wave, we sway and sway,
Chasing clouds in playful fray!

Liquid lullabies take flight,
Through the tides, what pure delight!
A symphony in laughter’s name,
Where joy and fun are never lame!

The Symphony of Liquid Moments

In the stream where laughter flows,
Silly thoughts like watercress grows.
Wiggly fish with hats swim by,
Tickling toes and making us sigh.

Waves applaud the jumpy frogs,
As they leap 'round floating logs.
Each ripple dances, a merry tune,
While ducks wear shades beneath the moon.

Giggling leaves in a swirling spree,
Whisper jokes to the bumblebee.
This playful scene, a liquid jest,
Shows nature's heart is at its best.

So grab a cup and fill it high,
With laughter's brew, don't be shy.
In this symphony of wet delight,
Dance with life till falls the night.

Tiny Visions in the Vastness

In a sea of thoughts that fizz and pop,
Tiny dreams begin to hop.
With every splash and every cheer,
Imagination's ship draws near.

Drifting boats made of candy floss,
Sailing on a wave, what a toss!
Squirrels on surfboards, what a scene,
Laughing at the world, so serene.

A whale wearing glasses, oh what flair!
Tells stories of jellyfish in midair.
While bubbles giggle, they rise and burst,
In this vastness, we quench our thirst.

So let's embrace the funny tide,
Where silly spirits dance and glide.
In every droplet, humor waits,
Tiny visions at joyful gates.

Fluid Fables Dancing at Dusk

As sunlight dips and shadows play,
Fluid fables swirl and sway.
A rainbow fish spins tales so bright,
While crickets clap to the fading light.

Dancing beams on the water's face,
Each ripple wears a smiling grace.
Tiny turtles in a cha-cha queue,
Making a splash beneath the blue.

With giggling waves that tickle our toes,
And laughter that everywhere flows.
A mermaid sings, with a wiggle and whirl,
Enchanting all in her glittering pearl.

So let the dusk bring tales of fun,
As the day bows low, its work well done.
Fluid fables blink in twilight's hush,
Where joyous echoes and starlight brush.

The Magic of Ephemeral Currents

A wink of light on a fleeting spree,
Lifts our spirits, sets us free.
Twisting rivers on a giggle ride,
Holding secrets with every stride.

Flip-flopping fish tell jokes so grand,
Splashing truths, laughter unplanned.
While crabs in socks march to a beat,
Their sideways shuffle can’t be beat.

As currents twist like a playful dog,
Chasing bubbles, like a quick fog.
Every moment a spark of cheer,
In this magic, we shed a tear.

So follow the flow, let joy increase,
In ephemeral currents, find your peace.
Let the tide of laughter ring,
In this wondrous world, let your heart sing.

Melodies of the Fluid World

In the stream where giggles flow,
Fish wear hats and dance in tow.
Splashing tunes, the frogs all croak,
While turtles tell the funniest joke.

Water lilies sway and spin,
A merry band where fin meets fin.
Driftwood guitars strum a tune,
As minnows tap beneath the moon.

Crickets chirp a silly beat,
While otters juggle tiny treats.
Ripples twirl like laughter's stream,
In this whimsical, watery dream.

So let the waves bring joy and cheer,
With each splash, a laugh draws near.
In fluid worlds, the fun won't cease,
Every moment, pure release.

Whirling Treasures beneath the Sky

Under clouds, the antics play,
Crabs wear sunglasses, bright and gay.
Dancing shells in a sandy waltz,
Playful seahorses cause swift halts.

The sunbeams tickle each fin and scale,
Clownfish tell jokes, they never fail.
Drifting starfish, in lazy cheer,
Join the frolic in the sapphire sphere.

Snails race by in a living blur,
As jellyfish sway, their colors stir.
The world below is a laughing spree,
In this merry realm, so wild and free.

With laughter echoing through the tides,
The ocean's silliness abides.
Every ripple, a joyous delight,
In the treasure trove of day and night.

Serene Circles in Gentle Currents

Where the water twirls and spins,
Giggling ducks wear rubber fins.
A chorus of ripples, soft and sweet,
In secret games, they never cheat.

The otter slides with a silly grin,
While frogs enjoy a splashy win.
Leaves like boats drift with pride,
All the creatures giggle and glide.

Laughter echoes from the banks,
As beavers build their playful pranks.
Every swirl an echo of glee,
In the serene circle of jubilee.

So let the waters laugh and play,
In the gentle flow of a sunny day.
A world of joy beneath the skies,
Where endless fun forever lies.

Light Constellations on a Liquid Canvas

In twilight hues the waters shine,
Frogs in tuxedos sip on brine.
A canvas stretched with giggles and glee,
Stars jump into the waves with glee.

The moonbeams paint the ripples high,
As shimmering fish leap to say hi.
A prankster eel does a wiggly dance,
And the wise old crab claims his chance.

Soft splashes in a starry night,
Whimsical dreams take joyous flight.
Each bubble of laughter lights the dark,
Creating constellations, a giggly spark.

Here beneath a starlit roof,
All the creatures goof and spoof.
With every flicker and glimmering wave,
In this playful world, we're all brave.

A Dance of Forthcoming Delight

In a stream where giggles laugh,
Fish wear hats and dance in half.
Rolling waves like jolly jest
Splashing joy, it's quite the fest.

Little feet on lily pads,
Skipping over giggling lads.
Sunlight twinkles, shadows play,
Nature's circus on display.

Amidst the weeds, a frog does sing,
Jumping high, a perfect fling.
Laughter ripples through the air,
Join us now, if you dare!

With every splash, the world ignites,
Colors twist as joy invites.
Nature's pranks in every turn,
In this dance, we all will learn.

Celestial Dreams Drift in the Stream.

Stars fall down like jelly beans,
Swirling softly, floating scenes.
Clouds above put on their show,
As the river starts to flow.

Wishes travel on the tide,
With a wink, they slip and glide.
Frogs in tuxedos congregate,
Laughing where the waters resonate.

Fish wear sunglasses, so divine,
Pose for photos, sip on brine.
Every splash a burst of cheer,
To the rhythm, draw us near.

Stars above and giggles round,
Echos of a joyous sound.
In this dream, let's drift away,
Let the stream decide our play.

Whispers on the Water

Waves are whispering silly glee,
Telling tales of fishy spree.
Loggers dance on twinkling light,
While crickets sing into the night.

Leaves are giggling, swaying free,
As they watch from every tree.
Water beetles, disco kings,
Spin and twirl on fragile wings.

Dance of currents, playful tease,
Nature laughing, if you please.
Every droplet tells a joke,
In the stream where spirits poke.

With a splash and gleeful wink,
Join the whispers, don’t you think?
Find the joy within the drift,
It's the universe’s gift.

Silent Swirls of Reflection

Mirror lakes with giggles sweep,
As fish beneath the surface leap.
Calm reflections twist and shout,
With every ripple, dance about.

Sun-kissed ripples chase the breeze,
Floating dreams like cotton cheese.
Ducks are snickering in a row,
While turtles move at half the flow.

In this whirl of silent fun,
Peace and laughter weave as one.
Every echo holds a dream,
Silly moments in the stream.

Round they go, this merry chase,
Splashing joy, a lively race.
If you listen close and clear,
You'll hear the giggles drawing near.

Shining Whispers from Below

In the pool of silly dreams,
Little thoughts swim and gleam.
Swirling giggles, round and bright,
Whispers dance in morning light.

Tiny voices make a splash,
Tickle toes with a splashy crash.
Laughter floats on waves of cheer,
Giddy sounds that bring us near.

Around the bends, they twirl away,
Chasing joys that tease and play.
A drop of fun, a swirl of glee,
Waving hello to you and me.

Who knew thoughts could dive and prance?
Join the party, take a chance!
With every giggle, rise and spin,
Life's a ride—let's dive right in!

Catching Moments in the Wake

Skimming stones on lazy streams,
Catching sparkles, wild and free.
Every ripple holds a joke,
As the water starts to poke.

Fishes leap with joyful squeaks,
Playing tricks on silly peaks.
Giggles chase the wake we make,
Wobbling like a wiggly cake.

Splashes echo, laughter swells,
In each bubble, a secret dwells.
Chasing thoughts like darting fish,
Every moment, a giddy wish.

When the world is upside down,
We take a turn, we spin around.
In the waves, we find our cake,
Catch the fun, make no mistake!

Harmony in Water’s Laughter

Ripples sing a merry tune,
Dancing 'neath the bright, full moon.
Giggling streams, a joyful flow,
Whirling round in splashes low.

Joyful gurgles, bubbling dreams,
Silly antics as it seems.
Water tickles with its touch,
Every swirl says, 'Not too much!'

With each twist, a secret peek,
Whispers soft, “You're all unique!”
Harmonies of fun unite,
In the waves, everything's right.

As the currents play their game,
We join in with laughter’s name.
Flow with cheer, let worries flee,
In this dance, forever free!

Shifting Spheres of Hope

Round and round, a playful glide,
Curves and arcs, a cheeky ride.
Spheres of joy on currents play,
Twisting through the light of day.

Hope floats high on cotton dreams,
Giddy spins and giggly beams.
Life's a game, let's roll the dice,
Balance wobbles—who's more nice?

Melodies in waves we find,
Silly echoes, hearts aligned.
With each shimmer, laughter grows,
In this dance, the happiness flows.

Let them roll, those sparks of light,
Shifting spheres, a pure delight.
Drawing us into a sweet cheer,
In every spin, our hearts are clear!

Secrets of Light on Fluid Surfaces

Glimmers dance and laugh in play,
Shimmering tricks in the light of day.
Droplets giggle, they jump and swirl,
Chasing reflections in a merry whirl.

Each flicker tells a witty tale,
Of water's pranks, a slippery trail.
Ripples share secrets with a wink,
Of swimsuits lost and drinks that stink.

Sunlight tickles where shadows hide,
Colors burst forth in joyful pride.
An afternoon’s jaunt, a playful tease,
Floating laughter on a gentle breeze.

Hey there, look—it's a watery jest!
A splash of whimsy, nature's best.
With every lurch, the liquid glows,
In these antics, laughter flows.

Melodies of the Wandering Orbs

Orbs of color, they leap and trot,
Singing tunes, in merry thought.
A jolly jig on rippling waves,
Whirling wonders that one behaves.

Tickle the surface, coax a sigh,
Watch them drift and whirl nearby.
Tiny giggles in blobs so round,
Floating cheer is always found.

With every pop what joy will rise!
A spectacle right before our eyes.
In the aquatic, laughter's muse,
Wandering orbs in joyful cruise.

With frothy tunes they spin and glide,
Bouncing along with joyful pride.
Nature's jesters, so merry and free,
They sing out loud—come dance with me!

Luminescence in the Submerged World

Where fishy friends wear coats that shine,
Glow and shimmer, oh how divine!
Giggling lights in the deep blue sea,
Winking at creatures, come play with me!

Underwater jesters, a radiant show,
Flipping and flopping, putting on a glow.
With every flick of their glorious fins,
Sparkling laughter, where fun begins.

A tidal wave of giggles roams,
From coral caves to aquatic homes.
Cheeky and bright, they swirl and sway,
Under the surface, night and day.

So dive right in, don't be shy,
Join the fun as the sea creatures fly.
With luminescence wrapping the scene,
Life's a party in colors unseen.

Porcelain Dreams on a Liquid Frontier

A porcelain cup tipped over the edge,
Dreams spill forth on a water pledge.
Singing softly, they float away,
Whispers of laughter at play all day.

Ripples giggle in a playful stream,
Chasing the shadows of an evening beam.
Lively shapes, they bounce and twirl,
Sliding on waves—a glassy whirl.

In a world of dreams where splashes giggle,
Witty wonders cause hearts to wiggle.
With every splash, smile wide and bright,
As porcelain dreams dance into the night.

So join the revel, let spirits lift,
Liquid delights, nature's playful gift.
In this playful mess, we twirl and prance,
Cherishing moments that make us dance.

Floating Dreams in Liquid Embrace

In a wobbly waltz, they spin and sway,
Bouncing around like they're at play.
With giggles and wiggles, they hop on the crest,
Escaping their worries, they give it their best.

A splash here, a splash there, oh what a sight,
They wobble and tumble, full of delight.
As laughter erupts from the shimmering glint,
They bubble with joy, and their spirits imprint.

Each twist of the tide brings a fresh new glee,
As they play hide and seek with a fish, oh so free.
With a wink and a nod, they dance in the light,
Spinning in circles, what a comical sight.

When the water is warm and the sun shines bright,
These merry little spheres float in delight.
With playful intentions, they bounce, twirl, and gleam,
In a world of pure joy, they live out their dream.

Ephemeral Orbs of the Stream

Across the stream, they flicker and glide,
With wiggles so silly, they take us for a ride.
Like tiny balloons in a playful ballet,
They giggle and shimmer, then drift far away.

Sipping on sunshine, they twinkle and tease,
Tickling the fish as they float with such ease.
In a soap suds parade, they frolic and play,
Mixing with laughter, lifting spirits each day.

Oh, how they glisten with mischievous flair!
Dancing on currents without a care.
Each orb a secret, a chuckle untold,
In this watery whirligig, daring and bold.

With whispers of mischief, they scatter with grace,
Leaving ripples of joy in their ephemeral race.
Chasing the sunlight, they swirl and they gleam,
In the playful embrace of a liquid daydream.

Dance of the Effervescent Waves

Effervescent whispers ripple on through,
As they twirl and tumble, all drenched in blue.
With giddy enthusiasm, they pop and they roar,
Bringing a fiesta to the ocean’s dance floor.

Jumping in sync with the rhythm so sweet,
Each bubble a boogie, a fizzling beat.
In this frothy lagoon, where laughter's the theme,
They twine and they swirl in a quirky daydream.

Splashing each other like toddlers at play,
With giggles erupting as they drift away.
A chorus of cheer, in the sea they unite,
Creating a carnival, pure joy in sight.

With a flip and a float, they frolic and fly,
Making waves in a jolly, bubbly sky.
This liquid fiesta, where humor's the rave,
Is the dance of the waves, oh so oddly brave.

Transient Spheres in Flow

In the swirl of the eddies, they bounce with glee,
As whimsical orbs, so fancy and free.
With a pop and a giggle, they soar through the air,
Leaving laughter behind, like bubbles with flair.

They twinkle at twilight, a frivolous sight,
Glistening brightly with mischief so light.
In a playful parade, they ride on the tide,
Chasing the winds where the silly dreams glide.

With a giggle and jiggle, they shimmy and shake,
Creating a ruckus—it's just what they make.
Each fleeting moment, a jest in the flow,
These transient spheres put on a grand show.

As night meets the day, they sparkle and laugh,
Carving out giggles, the best kind of path.
With their lighthearted dance, they banish the grim,
Floating along in their effervescent whim.

Glinting Joys in the Flowing Tide

A fish with shades swims through the blue,
Wearing a grin, it knows just what to do.
With a flip and a splash, it starts to play,
Tickling the seaweed, making spirits sway.

Crabs breakdance on the sandy floor,
While seahorses giggle, calling out for more.
A starfish whispers jokes to a clam,
Laughter echoes, a delightful jam.

Jellyfish wobble like balloons in flight,
Dancing through currents, a whimsical sight.
They bob and weave, with slack and tension,
Spreading joy in their watery dimension.

With bubbles of joy and a splash of glee,
Every creature joins in for the jubilee.
The tide rolls in, full of gleeful delight,
In this cheerful show, everything feels right.

Ebbing Laughter in the Stream

In a bustling brook, the minnows race,
Chasing each other, a slippery chase.
They giggle and skip over pebbly ground,
A ticklish sensation, laughter profound.

A frog leaps high, with a croaky cheer,
Telling the fish they should come near.
With a big belly flop, he lands with a splash,
Sending ripples of giggles in a joyful flash.

Dragonflies hover, all wearing hats,
Buzzing around like delightful bats.
They trade silly jokes with the wise old heron,
As the laughter flows with an easy errand.

The willow tree chuckles, swaying in breeze,
Its branches whispering, "Oh, do as you please!"
With each little ripple, the joy multiplies,
A funny parade under sunny skies.

Soft Echoes of Nature’s Breath

A wooden duck floats on a mirror so clear,
Waving to turtles that cheer, “Come here!”
With feathers so shiny, it quacks like a pro,
Bouncing on currents, putting on a show.

Nearby, a squirrel attempts a tightrope,
Balancing acorns with much falter and hope.
With a tumble and giggle, it lands in a pile,
Causing a chorus of chuckles and smiles.

Clouds drift lazily, painting the sky,
A raccoon observes, rolling an eye.
He tosses out jokes, witty and spry,
Leaving the birds with a merry reply.

Nature’s soft echoes dance on the air,
Tickling the flowers, swaying with flair.
It twirls through the grass, a giddy little dream,
A playful reminder of joy’s gentle theme.

Radiant Spirits in the Flow

As the river laughs, it twirls and spins,
Inviting the frogs to join in their whims.
With belly flops and the splash of a fin,
Each ripple rejoices, letting fun begin.

A crowd of ducks waddles, quacking away,
Trading old stories with flair and display.
While turtles in hats cheer, “Oh, look at us!”
Creating a mess—oh, what a fuss!

Each breeze that passes brings giggles anew,
With whispers of trees, “Let’s join in too!”
Laughter flows freely, a musical tune,
In the heart of the current, beneath the moon.

The shimmering sparkles dance on the crest,
As creatures unite for a comedic fest.
In the river’s embrace, there's nothing but cheer,
Life’s a grand joke when we all gather near.

The Elusive Symphony of Rippling Air

In a dance of gusts, they prance,
Chasing whispers, a frolicsome chance.
Like silly puppets, up they soar,
Tickling the breezes, forevermore.

With childish glee, they swirl around,
Bouncing on currents, never bound.
Pop! A giggle escapes from small lips,
As skyward they tumble, on light trips.

A chase for laughter, they twirl and spin,
Like merry sprites with cheeky grins.
In the great ballet of airy flight,
Who knew the sky could be so light?

As they frolic, no care in the world,
Each twist and turn—joy unfurled.
An elusive symphony, oh what a sight,
In the giggling chase of pure delight!

Fragile Joys Amongst the Waves

Waves of laughter, softly they creep,
Amidst the chaos, secrets they keep.
Each little splash, a chuckle or two,
As frothy delights come into view.

Floating on dreams, the giggles rise,
Mirrored by sunlight in playful skies.
With ridiculous hopes, they bob and sway,
In the dance of tides, come what may.

Silly sprites in a splashy embrace,
Slipping and sliding, they quicken the pace.
Frothy delights with a wink and a jest,
In this grand ocean, they find their rest.

Joys so fragile, they shimmer and gleam,
Carried along, like our wildest dream.
Amongst the waves, they find their tone,
In the playful abyss, forever home.

Serendipitous Spheres in Motion

In a world of bounces, they leap and twirl,
Chasing the laughter, giving it a whirl.
Round and round in a whimsical chase,
Each little sphere finds its energetic space.

Sailing through sunlight, they giggle and glide,
In a riot of colors, they take a ride.
What joy and folly in every arc,
As they play tag with the light and the dark.

Popping and fizzing, they burst into cheer,
Whirling with wonder, no hint of fear.
Life's little orbs, so carefree and bright,
In their playful ballet, everything feels right.

Unruly dancers in laughter's embrace,
Flowing and bubbling, they set their pace.
Serendipity sings in their frolicking song,
In this carnival of joy, we all belong!

Reflections of the Tenacious Softness

Floating on laughter, so gentle and light,
Reflecting the joy in each playful flight.
With twinkling giggles, they fill up the air,
Echoing soft dreams, beyond compare.

A dance with the wind, oh what a tease,
Each roll and bounce brings us to our knees.
Delighting in softness, they flit and fly,
Drawing smiles from passersby in the sky.

Erasing worries with a flick and a spin,
A dance that invites you to just dive in.
With every swirl, they charm and beguile,
A world of soft whispers, wrapped in a smile.

Reflections of joy, elusive and sweet,
In the fabric of laughter, we all meet.
Tenacious softness, it fills up the span,
Making merry moments from whatever we can!

Nurtured by Currents

In a dance of the merry streams,
The fish wear hats, or so it seems.
They giggle as they twirl around,
Caught up in joy, completely unbound.

With waves that tickle and tease the tide,
They whisper secrets, nowhere to hide.
A splash of laughter, a shimmer of fun,
Each twist and turn, a wild run!

Underwater revelry, quite the show,
With critters of every shape in tow.
They ride the ripples, carefree and light,
Chasing the moonbeams, out of sight.

So here's to the currents, full of cheer,
Where fish wear smiles, oh so dear.
Let's dive in and join the spree,
In this kooky world, wild and free!

Born of Air

From the skies, a drop does fall,
In sudsy spirals, it takes its call.
A bubble born with dreams of flight,
Floating high, a whimsical sight.

It dances lightly on the breeze,
Tickling noses with utmost ease.
Like a soap parade, bright and bold,
In the sunlight, it's magic to behold.

But oh, the mischief it can bring,
As kids laugh out and cheer and sing.
Pops and splashes, a fizzy delight,
In realms where giggles reach new height.

Float away, dear sphere of glee,
A brief escape, then you’re free.
Each journey short, yet filled with cheer,
Born of air, you disappear!

The Silken Thread of Breathing Water

Treading softly on liquid threads,
Hand in hand with the riverbeds.
A silk ribbon glides, oh what a sight,
As fish tell stories, day turns to night.

With every ripple, a chuckle and cheer,
Where elves and sprites, they swim so near.
In the cool depths, mischief is rife,
Woven tales of undersea life.

They tug at the threads, and laughter bursts,
With splashes and swirls, they're quenched of thirst.
A tapestry spun in wavy delight,
Stitched with joy, it’s pure dynamite!

So come join this frolicsome spree,
In silken patterns, we’ll feel so free.
Celebrate the dance, the push and pull,
In the realm of water, the heart is full!

Ethereal Alchemy of Fluid Whispers

In shimmering pools, whispers collide,
Like giggles shared on a joyous ride.
Each drop a secret, each splash a jest,
Ethereal magic, truly the best.

Mixing the hues, a painter's delight,
With laughter that twirls in purest flight.
A concoction of whimsy, oh so bright,
Fluid whispers dance in the moonlight.

Waves that chuckle, tides that play,
With a wink and smile, they steal the day.
So here on the surface, we'll buoy the laugh,
In the alchemy of joy, we'll chart our path!

So swirl with me in this liquid jest,
In watery realms where we're truly blessed.
With each little drop, let happiness flow,
In this sea of giggles, we steal the show!

Cascading Color in the Deep

In the depths where colors collide,
A symphony of shades, what a ride!
Fish dressed in rainbows, a sight to behold,
With stories of secrets, and treasures untold.

Swirls and patterns, a painter's glee,
As currents transport joy endlessly.
With paintbrushes made from fins that gleam,
Crafting laughter like a waking dream.

A canvas of motion, oh so vast,
Where tickles of water are meant to last.
Through moods and hues that twist and leap,
In depths of mirth, our souls take a peep.

So cherish the colors as they cascade,
In the watery realm where fun is made.
Join in the laughter, share the swim,
In this brilliant sea, let your light never dim!

Timeless Raindrops in the Flowing Sea

In a rush, they swirl and spin,
Like tiny boats with nobody in.
Laughing softly as they go,
Playing tag in the ebb and flow.

They slip and slide, oh what a sight,
Dancing round in pure delight.
Chasing shadows, making haste,
A jolly race with no time to waste.

Seashells hiding, grinning wide,
As they watch the droplets glide.
Tiny friends with a playful gleam,
Weaving their way through a daydream.

Tickling toes and leaving trails,
Whispering stories in the gales.
When the sun dips down for a chat,
The giggles rise, imagine that!

Liquid Memories

Splashing colors on a whim,
Frolicking in the water's rim.
They chase the fish, they tease the tide,
In a realm where joy can’t hide.

Wiggly tails and flip-flop sounds,
Bouncing off the sandy grounds.
The waves just chuckle, soft and low,
As the giggling droplets flow.

A tiny splash, a rippling cheer,
Echoes of laughter we hold dear.
In the depths, the secrets hide,
Bouncing about, they can’t abide.

With every splash, a memory made,
Worthy of a joyful parade.
Charmed by the sunlight’s golden kiss,
They dance with glee, what bliss is this?

Softly Whispered

Gentle whispers, sweet and light,
Tickle the surface, teasing sight.
Tickling waves with all their might,
A giggly dance through day and night.

Each ripple tells a funny tale,
A splash, a hug, a watery pail.
Thankful fish give a cheeky grin,
As they join the jolly din.

The sunbeams wink from high above,
Sending down a ray of love.
While drips and drops collide with glee,
Unfolding laughter at their spree.

With each plop, a joy proclaimed,
In the theater of water, they're untamed.
The current laughs and skips along,
In this sappy, swirling song.

Unseen Dreams in the Gentle Drift

Whispers swirl into the blue,
Chasing treasures, with a view.
Floating softly, they sneak away,
Into the waves where dreams can play.

Silly knots and swirling fates,
Making friends with funny mates.
Seashells giggle in the spray,
As unseen wishes drift and sway.

Dancing lightly, a flicker bright,
They bounce and jive, a funny sight.
Beneath the waves, a comical scene,
Where nothing's serious, just routine.

Each ripple holds a chuckle vast,
While yesterdays and tomorrows blast.
A parade of joy in playful prose,
Where laughter blooms and mischief grows.

Floating Echoes of Yesterday

Echoing laughter from days of yore,
Drifting softly to the shore.
With a giggle and a splashy cheer,
The past and future dance quite near.

In soft swirls, the moments glide,
Sailing gently like summer's tide.
Frolicking freely without a care,
In a sea of whispers, everywhere.

Lunar light plays peek-a-boo,
With every wave, a playful view.
Silly fish join the caper too,
As the playful dreams come into view.

Comical echoes twirl and tease,
Turning memories into breezy ease.
Splashing tales that feel so sly,
Where laughter reigns and spirits fly.

Breathless Hues in the Liquid Flow

A splash of laughter paints the stream,
Colors dancing, giggles gleam.
Wobbly wonders float with glee,
Wiggly whirls, oh look at me!

A swirl of joy, a fizzy sound,
Bouncing high, then falling down.
Each little plop, a playful tease,
Chasing dreams with wobbly ease.

The river sings, a song of cheer,
Silly sighs, the fish draw near.
Riding waves on laughter’s tide,
With every flip, a silly slide!

Sipping sunshine, tasting the breeze,
In this dance, we bend our knees.
A vibrant trickle, a jolly chase,
Splashing smiles, all over the place!

Secrets Wrapped in Liquid Veils

Hidden giggles swim around,
In murky depths, fun is found.
Whispers of joy, they jiggle and jive,
As fish in tutu's start to thrive.

Mysterious splashes spark delight,
With every pop, a playful fright.
Under the surface, secrets spin,
Where crabs wear crowns and turtles grin.

Liquid mysteries twist and turn,
In this crazy realm, we laugh and learn.
A swirling dance, all things collide,
With rubber duckies, we take a ride!

The current tickles, a teasing race,
Water games, let's set the pace.
Bouncing ripples, giggling waves,
Join the fun where silliness saves!

Flickering Fantasies on Rippling Waters

Glittering dreams on swirling paths,
Chasing shadows, with silly laughs.
Float along, no worries here,
With wiggly worms, we conquer fear.

Waves break out in chuckles bright,
Every dip, a pure delight.
Plinky plonks on the softest crest,
Where frogs join in for a ribbit fest.

A frothy giggle, a twirling bound,
Water sprites leap, joy profound.
Tickling toes, a slippery ride,
With every splash, we laugh and slide!

Wiggly wonders in poolside rays,
Playing hopscotch in sunlit bays.
With fishy friends, we sing along,
In this liquid land where we belong!

Crystalline Dreams Dipped in Light

Glistening paths where sparkles play,
Water droplets dance, hip-hip hooray!
Gliding light on a velvet floor,
Magic flips, we all want more!

Shiny wishes float and spin,
With giggles loud, let's dive in!
Tickled pink by the playful glow,
Frothy fountains, on the go!

Jumpy twists in the sunshine's kiss,
Each splash whipped up a liquid bliss.
Gurgling laughter fills the air,
In this chaos, we've naught a care!

A shimmering swirl, a tickle spree,
Under the sea, we giggle free.
With watery winks, we dream tonight,
In crystalline realms dipped in light!

The Surrender of Air to Water

In a puddle, splashes fly,
A fish jumps up, oh my, oh my!
With a laugh, the water grins,
As the bubble pops and spins.

Air came down, quite ill-prepared,
Only to find a party shared.
A splash here, a giggle there,
Oh look! A duck in underwear!

The raindrops dance like silly mates,
Making beats as they celebrate.
Who knew that floating could be fun?
With every wave, their joy's begun.

So let the stream hold quips and quirks,
As we share our laughing smirks.
In the waters, joy will sway,
Together we'll splash the day away.

Enchanted Dance of the Damp Breeze

The breeze tickles, oh so sly,
It whispers low, then zooms on by.
Leaves shimmy with a little prance,
As raindrops join the cheeky dance.

Each droplet laughs, a merry chime,
They spin and twirl, they bide their time.
Through the trees, the currents tease,
With breezy chuckles, hearts they please.

Fish flip-flop, a wet ballet,
Their fins like ribbons in the spray.
Butterflies join in the fun,
Oh how nature loves to run!

So let's sway with every gust,
And find pure joy in damp, we trust.
In this dance where laughter flows,
Life is grand, as everyone knows!

Fleeting Echoes of the Waters' Embrace

A turtle spins, all in a whirl,
While giggling minnows chime and twirl.
The river chuckles, “Catch me quick!”
But all it does is play a trick.

As boats bob in a gentle race,
A lone frog joins with style and grace.
“Ribbit-Ribbit!” it cheers aloud,
The water sways, feeling proud.

Each ripple brings a chuckling cheer,
Sharing secrets only we hear.
“Oh what fun!” the river proclaims,
As it splashes back with no shame.

Thus we ride this joyful stream,
With laughter flowing as our theme.
In the water's arms, we’re free,
Embracing joy with glee and glee!

Iridescent Secrets of the Flowing Stream

Glittering trails weave through the clay,
While slippery eels perform ballet.
They wiggle and giggle, a sight so bright,
Chasing sunbeams, pure delight.

The stones chuckle under the dance,
As ripples skip, a merry prance.
“Who’s splashy now?” the water teases,
With every spray, laughter pleases.

Fish tickle toes that dip too low,
Water sprites join in the show.
“Oh my!” we shout with every lurch,
While the current leads us on, we search.

So sip this nectar of joyful waves,
In the laughter of a stream that saves.
Where secrets gleam, and smiles are born,
Dive right in; let joy adorn!

www.ingramcontent.com/pod-product-compliance
Lightning Source LLC
Chambersburg PA
CBHW060143230426
43661CB00003B/549
9781805872467